SCOTTISH FREIGHT-ONLY LINES

MIKE MACDONALD

PENNINE PUBLICATIONS LTD.
SHEFFIELD

Price: £2·45

First published 1985

© Pennine Publications Ltd. 1985

SBN 946055 05 X

All photographs are from the Author's Collection, unless otherwise credited

Front Cover:
The Granton branch (Lothian). 26 036 at Granton with the Inspection Saloon on 13/10/1983.
(Douglas Blades)

Printed in Great Britain
by
Waddington & Sons (Printers) Ltd.
Fielden Square, Todmorden, Lancs. OL14 7LE

INTRODUCTION

THIS booklet aims to be useful to the railway enthusiast. To that end, it illustrates all the freight-only lines in Scotland (except Ministry of Defence lines) which have regular freight workings on them, together with one or two lines which are only occasionally (or rarely) used.

The photographic captions give (1) the Ordnance Survey 1:50,000 (Second Series) sheet numbers for the photographic locations; (2) the National Grid Reference Numbers for the locations; (3) a general idea of the time of day when the photograph was taken; (4) the *approximate* regularity of the service, and (5) some general "background" about the freight workings illustrated. Where appropriate, there are cross-references, when the opposite ends of workings are illustrated in different parts of the booklet. The photographs are arranged geographically from North to South and a sketch map is provided.

The pattern of freight traffic in Scotland is changing all the time, as redundant facilities and lines are closed. Recently, there have been dramatic changes in the appearance of Millerhill and Bathgate, and, late in 1984, it was rumoured that the Annbank-Mauchline line in Strathclyde would close.

Some types of traffic wax or wane as consumer demand changes. Because of a fall in sales of Scotch whisky, grain traffic has declined at locations like Inverhouse, Burghead and Dufftown. On the other hand, new opportunities may open up as a result of Government grants made under the Railways Act of 1974. As a result of one such grant, export coal traffic was resumed at Leith Docks in 1981, and similar grants were made to inaugurate, improve or restore rail handling facilities at Ayr Harbour, Bathgate, Dalry, Garsherrie, Greenock (Clyde Port Authority), Inverhouse, Keith, and a number of other locations.

Another interesting development has been the growing co-operation between British Rail and various road haulage and storage firms. A number of "break-bulk" storage and distribution depots have been set up, at Deanside, Grangemouth, Law Junction, Mossend, and elsewhere. Trunk haulage from England is provided by the railways and local distribution performed by the road hauliers.

It proved impossible to obtain photographs of contemporary motive power on all lines, but there were some excellent (and rare) photographs of some lines from steam days, and I have included them.

I would like to thank the following for their help in preparing this booklet: James Stevenson, Stuart Sellar, Bill Roberton, Bill Hamilton and James Currie, who kindly allowed me to use some of their photographs; Douglas Blades, who took some photographs for me on request; Stuart Sellar, who read over the Introduction and captions; and Therese Macdonald, for putting up with it all.

MIKE MACDONALD
Dalmeny, West Lothian.

November, 1984.

1. **GRAMPIAN REGION.** Aberdeen (Waterloo Branch). OS38; NJ936074.
The Waterloo branch drops steeply from Kittybrewster to the quayside at Waterloo, site of the original passenger terminus in Aberdeen. It is now the British Steel Corporation's pipe depot for North Sea oil servicing.
08 828 was making its way round some sinuous trackwork on its return to Kittybrewster on the morning of 14/6/1984. The bolster wagons had delivered pipe manufactured at Coatbridge (see also 44).
(M. Macdonald)

2. **GRAMPIAN.** Aberdeen Harbour lines. OS38; NJ945061.
The Aberdeen Harbour lines, though still in place, are little used. 0-4-0ST *City of Aberdeen* (Black, Hawthorn; 1887) was on a tour of the lines on 11/10/1969.
(J. L. Stevenson)

3 & 4.　GRAMPIAN REGION.　The North of Scotland Whisky lines.
3.　Keith-Dufftown. OS28; NJ406468.
Traffic on the Whisky lines is now sparse because of the drop in the demand for Scotch whisky. British Rail ran a number of "Northern Belle" specials from Aberdeen to Dufftown to visit the Glenfiddich Distillery. 47 598 headed one of these on 13/6/1984, seen here near Auchindachy. Until recently, malted barley was forwarded from Inverhouse (see 43), but there is now no regular traffic.
(M. Macdonald)

4. GRAMPIAN.   Alves Junction-Burghead. OS28; NJ117690.
There are two bulk grain terminals on the Burghead branch, at Burghead and Roseisle, but traffic is variable.
    Highland Railway "Jones Goods" 4-6-0 No. 103 was seen at Burghead on the "Scottish Rambler" rail tour on 21/4/1962. *(W. S. Sellar)*

5. TAYSIDE.   Dundee Harbour. OS54; NO420308.
The lines at Dundee Harbour, like those at Aberdeen, are now little used. North British Locomotive Company shunter 11708 was working a train including bitumen tanks from the tar works on 3/10/1957.
(J. L. Stevenson)

7

6. FIFE. Thornton Junction-Methil Docks. OS59; NO379005.
The main rail-borne traffic through Methil Docks is imported wood pulp. 20 202 was leaving Methil in the early afternoon of 4/7/1984 on the daily trip back to Thornton. The train consisted of wagons of pulp for the paper mill at Corpach (Fort William); the wagons went forward on the Thornton-Mossend Speedlink working that evening. (See also 39.)
    Methil Power Station (background) is supplied with coal from a number of local sites. (See also 7, 8 and 12.)   *(M. Macdonald)*

7. FIFE. Thornton (Section Siding). OS59; NT290972.
A coal train for Methil Power Station (6), photographed on 14/3/1983 between Thornton (Section Siding) (formerly Thornton Yard) and Thornton Junction, with 20 149 in charge.   *(M. Macdonald)*

8. FIFE. Thornton (Section Siding)-Westfield. OS58; NT210977.
The Westfield branch passes through some pleasantly countrified parts of Central Fife en route to the Westfield Open Cast Coal Disposal Point. An enthusiasts' special visited the branch on 16/6/1984.
Westfield normally supplies coal slurry to Longannet (10) and Methil (6) Power Stations.
(M. Macdonald)

9. FIFE. Markinch-Auchmuty Mill. OS59; NO284015.
The notice says it all! The rail exit from the Tullis Russell Rothes Mill (under the A92 road) is a tight fit for 08 441, propelling a china clay hopper and pulling a load of empty coal wagons. 21/4/1982.
The china clay comes from Cornwall. The short wheelbase wagons are preferred to larger bogie hoppers for obvious reasons. (See also 39 and 49.) *(M. Macdonald)*

10. FIFE. Comrie Colliery Branch (NCB-owned spur from Dunfermline (Townhill)-Oakley line). OS65: NT021895. The noon trip from Comrie Colliery to Oakley sidings, crossing the Dunfermline-Alloa road on 8/10/1982 with 08 425 in charge. The branch is operated by NCB staff using 08s hired from British Rail. The train was conveying "Rexco" smokeless fuel from the Comrie plant (for domestic consumers) and "Comrie Filtercake" for Methil Power Station. (See 6, 7.) The Dunfermline-Oakley line formerly ran through to Alloa (see 17), but, by 1982, it had been closed and lifted west of Oakley. *(M. Macdonald)*

11 & 12. FIFE. Charlestown Junction-Longannet Power Station and Elbowend Junction-Crombie. OS65; NY072845.

11. Charlestown Junction-Longannet. NT089861.
Near Charlestown Junction (Dunfermline), 27 019 was on a train of ballast wagons on 13/9/1979. Since the "mothballing" of the Alloa-Kincardine line in 1981 (see 17), this line is now the only route to Longannet for coal trains from Fife (8) and the Lothians (32). *(M. Macdonald)*

12. Elbowend Junction-Crombie.
20 205 with a brakevan on 24/6/1983.

(M. Macdonald)

13. **FIFE. Kirkcaldy Harbour. OS59; NT285922.**
The Kirkcaldy Harbour incline (1 in 30) is one of the most steeply graded branches on British Rail. On 22/7/1983, 20 223 was propelling a pair of loaded 58-tonne capacity grain hoppers up the gradient. There is now no regular traffic on the branch, though, when the photograph was taken, there was seasonal (harvest times) traffic; this particular load was going to Ipswich. The branch was closed in October 1984.
(M. Macdonald)

14. Kirkcaldy Harbour again. The Class 06s worked the branch for a number of years, having taken over from the ex-North British Railway J88 0-6-0Ts. A rare photograph of No. 2442 on the branch on 10/9/1970.
(W. S. Sellar)

15. FIFE. Burntisland Harbour. OS66; NT235856.
There is still track at Burntisland Harbour, but it has seen little use since the British Alcan works at Burntisland ceased to receive imported bauxite by rail in 1982. 20 221 was shunting bauxite wagons (loaded from the barge in the background) on 13/9/1979.
(M. Macdonald)

16. FIFE. Inverkeithing-Inverkeithing Harbour and Rosyth Dockyard. OS65: NT132828.
Like the Kirkcaldy Harbour branch described above, this line drops away steeply from the main Edinburgh-Aberdeen line. 20 226 is seen climbing back to Inverkeithing with the daily early morning return trip to Thornton on 18/4/1983; the train includes some modern high-sided steel scrap wagons (POAs) from the harbour scrap yard.
There is a twice-daily unadvertised passenger service over the branch, to and from Kirkcaldy, for workers at Rosyth Dockyard.

(M. Macdonald)

17 & 18. CENTRAL. Stirling-Alloa via Cambus Junction and Cambus Junction-Menstrie.

17. OS57; NS839948.
This is the Western end of the former North British Railway Stirling-Alloa-Oakley-Dunfermline and Stirling-Alloa-Kincardine-Longannet-Charlestown Junction lines.
    20 115 is seen west of Cambus Junction on the "main line" in the early afternoon of 16/3/1983, returning to Grangemouth with empty molasses tanks. This is now the only regular traffic on the line; loaded molasses tanks are forwarded to the Glenochil Distillery at Menstrie from Greenock (see 58) or from British Sugar Corporation's works south of the border.
    The line from Alloa to Kincardine was "mothballed" in 1981, pending the redevelopment of the nearby Polmaise colliery, but, as the colliery's future is now in doubt, the line may not re-open.
(M. Macdonald)

18. OS58; NS849952.
Earlier on 16/3/1983, 20 115 was on the Menstrie branch, returning to Alloa with empty molasses tanks.
(M. Macdonald)

19. CENTRAL.   Falkirk-Grangemouth. OS65; NS900799.
This busy branch serves the Grangemouth Refinery and its associated petro-chemical works. There are a number of daily trains of petroleum products to distribution points in Central and Southern Scotland [Paisley (Hawkhead) (55); Dumfries (72); Leith (34)], and in Northern England. One of these trains, to Granton (38), now withdrawn, is seen approaching Falkirk on 3/4/1980 with 37 111 in charge.
(M. Macdonald)

20. CENTRAL.   Grangemouth Refinery. OS65; NS945825.
On the morning of 12/4/1983, 08 347 crosses the Dock Road into the Refinery sidings to deliver a tank of lead additive. *(M. Macdonald)*

21. **CENTRAL. Grangemouth. OS65; NS938822.**
British Petroleum's Barclay shunter brings chemical (1-Hexene) and petroleum tanks out to the British Rail Exchange Sidings on the morning of 5/7/1984. *(M. Macdonald)*

22. **CENTRAL. Grangemouth Docks. OS65; NS948828.**
Wagons of steel coil (for export to Italy) are shunted on the quayside at Grangemouth Docks by 08 196 on 24/1/1983. The steel was supplied by the British Steel Corporation's Gartcosh mill (see also 48). Grangemouth Docks were developed in the 1860s for the export of coal. Coal exports ceased in the 1960s, but coal imports continue, as the coal lorries in the photograph show. *(M. Macdonald)*

23. **CENTRAL.** Grangemouth (Fouldubs). OS65; NS916809. Many of the dockland sidings are now closed for lack of traffic, and the sidings at Fouldubs can handle the wagonload and non-oil traffic that remains. 37 112 is seen leaving Fouldubs just after noon on 19/5/1983 with a train of empty cement wagons for Oxwellmains (East Lothian). (See also 27.) *(M. Macdonald)*

24. CENTRAL. Grangemouth (Fouldubs)-Falkirk (Orchardhall). OS65; NS909809.
This line formerly joined the Falkirk (Grahamston) loop at a point just west of Grahamston station, but now it only runs as far as the aluminium works at Orchardhall. At the moment, the line is moribund, its future dependent on the transport needs of the works. In better days, 2F 0-6-0 57287 was seen leaving Fouldubs on the branch on 19/2/1949. *(J. L. Stevenson)*

25. CENTRAL. Falkirk (Grahamston Goods). OS65; NS891804.
This branch disappears round a sharp (180 degree) curve at the east end of Falkirk (Grahamston) station. The goods yard has accommodated the Central Scotland distribution depot of a firm of brickmakers from the English Midlands, but it is believed that this operation will be transferred elsewhere. 27 063 was shunting empty brick wagons at the yard on 5/7/1984. *(M. Macdonald)*

26. CENTRAL. Grangemouth (Fouldubs).
Fouldubs again, looking in the other direction. On 19/5/1983, 08 196 was propelling some PCA wagons beneath the M9 Motorway into the cement siding. Beside the cement siding is a rail/road "break-bulk" depot [see also Deanside (54)] which handles regular railway vanload traffic. The Orchardhall branch also goes off at this point.
(M. Macdonald)

LOTHIAN REGION. Edinburgh Area.
27. Monktonhall Junction-Millerhill. OS66; NT330708.
A cement train from Oxwellmains approaches Millerhill from the east on 8/4/1980 with 40 197 in charge. A number of cement trains pass through Millerhill daily in the afternoon and early evening. (See also 23, 24.) *(M. Macdonald)*

28. **LOTHIAN.** Millerhill (Section Siding) (formerly Millerhill Yard). OS66; NT321713.
One of the most photographed views in Scotland. On the early evening of 15/6/1983, 46 027 was leaving Millerhill on a Freightliner train, while 40 090 was waiting to enter the yard with a train of empty "Cartics" from Bathgate (41, 42) to Bescot. Millerhill, opened about 1960, is now much reduced in traffic and in status. In 1984, the whole "down" side and two of the four through running lines were closed and lifted. *(M. Macdonald)*

29. LOTHIAN. Edinburgh "Suburban" line ("The Sub"). (Niddrie West Junction-Haymarket West Junction/Slateford Junction). OS66; NT233713.
"The Sub" is an important freight route by-passing Edinburgh city centre to the south and west. At Craiglockhart Junction, on the west side of the city, 40 063 was taking the line to Haymarket West Junction with a cement train from Oxwellmains on 21/3/1980.
(*M. Macdonald*)

30. LOTHIAN. "The Sub".
Craiglockhart Junction, looking downhill towards Haymarket this time. 47 553 is seen on the chord from Slateford Junction on the afternoon of 9/8/1978 with a Glasgow (Gushetfaulds)-Edinburgh (Portobello) Freightliner train.
  "The Sub" lost its passenger services in 1962. Various road building proposals involving the "conversion" (or breach) of "The Sub" have (so far) come to nothing. *(M. Macdonald)*

31. LOTHIAN. "The Sub". OS66; NT228718.
Further down the hill from Craiglockhart (30) is the site of the former Gorgie Market Junction. On 3/7/1978, 40 061 was heading for Haymarket while 26 007 was coming uphill, en route for Millerhill, with a short train of tanks.
  Until the early 1960s, sidings went off at this point; left into the Gorgie Markets; right into a bonded warehouse. *(M. Macdonald)*

32. LOTHIAN. Millerhill Junction-Bilston Glen Colliery. OS66; NT317690.
Bilston Glen Colliery supplies coal to the Power Station at Cockenzie (East Lothian), and also coal for export through Leith Docks (see 33). 26 006 is shown in 1977 with an afternoon "merry-go-round" train for Cockenzie. *(M. Macdonald)*

33. LOTHIAN. Leith Docks. OS66; NT280765.
A modern coal loader was commissioned at Leith Docks in 1981, allowing coal exports to be resumed after a gap of several years. 26 007 was at the loader on 28/5/1981 with coal for Copenhagen. Coal is supplied from Bilston Glen (32) and from Blindwells Open Cast Site (East Lothian). Between four and six trains may run in one day, but the traffic is variable. *(M. Macdonald)*

Scottish Freight-Only Lines

KEY TO THE MAP

The representation on this map of any freight line does not imply that there will be a freight working on that line on any given day.

GRAMPIAN REGION
1. Aberdeen, Waterloo branch
2. Aberdeen, Harbour
3. Dufftown branch
4. Burghead branch

TAYSIDE REGION
5. Dundee Harbour

FIFE REGION
6. Methil branch
7. Thornton (Section Siding)
8. Westfield branch
9. Auchmuty branch
10. Longannet branch
11. Crombie branch
12. Comrie Colliery branch
13. Kirkcaldy Harbour
14. Kirkcaldy Harbour
15. Burntisland Harbour
16. Rosyth Dockyard branch

CENTRAL REGION
17. Stirling-Alloa
18. Menstrie branch
19. Grangemouth branch
20. Grangemouth Refinery
21. Grangemouth B.P. Chemicals
22. Grangemouth Docks
23. Grangemouth Fouldubs
24. Grangemouth Fouldubs
25. Grangemouth Orchardhall branch
26. Falkirk Grahamston (Goods)

LOTHIAN REGION (Edinburgh Area)
27. Monktonhall Jct.-Millerhill
28. Millerhill (Section Siding)
29. "The Sub"
30. "The Sub"
31. "The Sub"
32. Bilston Glen branch
33. Leith Docks
34. Leith Docks (Unitank)
35. Leith Docks
36. Leith South (Goods)
37. Leith South Junction
38. Granton branch

LOTHIAN REGION (outside Edinburgh)
39. Dalmeny-Winchburgh
40. Polkemmet Colliery
41. Bathgate
42. Bathgate

STRATHCLYDE REGION (Airdrie-Coatbridge-Mossend-Motherwell)
43. Inverhouse (Airdrie)
44. B.S.C. Imperial ("Calder") branch
45. Whifflet-Coatbridge (Sunnyside)-Gunnie
46. Gartsherrie Cement Works
47. Rutherglen Jct.-Rosehall Jct.
48. Ravenscraig Steel Works
49. Mossend Yard
50. Holytown Jct.-Law Jct.
51. Coltness branch

STRATHCLYDE REGION (Glasgow (South))
52. Larkfield Junction
53. General Terminus
54. Deanside branch
55. Paisley (Hawkhead)

STRATHCLYDE REGION (Glasgow (North))
56. Dalmuir Riverside branch
57. High Street Junction

STRATHCLYDE REGION
58. Greenock Docks
59. Greenock Princes Pier

STRATHCLYDE REGION (Ayrshire)
60. Giffen branch
61. Dalry (Roche Products)
62. Ardrossan (Shell refinery)
63. Ardrossan (Shell refinery)
64. Dubbs Jct.-Byrehill Jct.
65. Snodgrass, Bogside
66. Ayr Harbour
67. Killoch Colliery branch
68. Annbank Jct.-Mauchline Jct.
69. Waterside branch
70. Kilmarnock (Riccarton)
71. Barony Colliery

DUMFRIES AND GALLOWAY REGION
72. Dumfries (Maxwelltown branch)

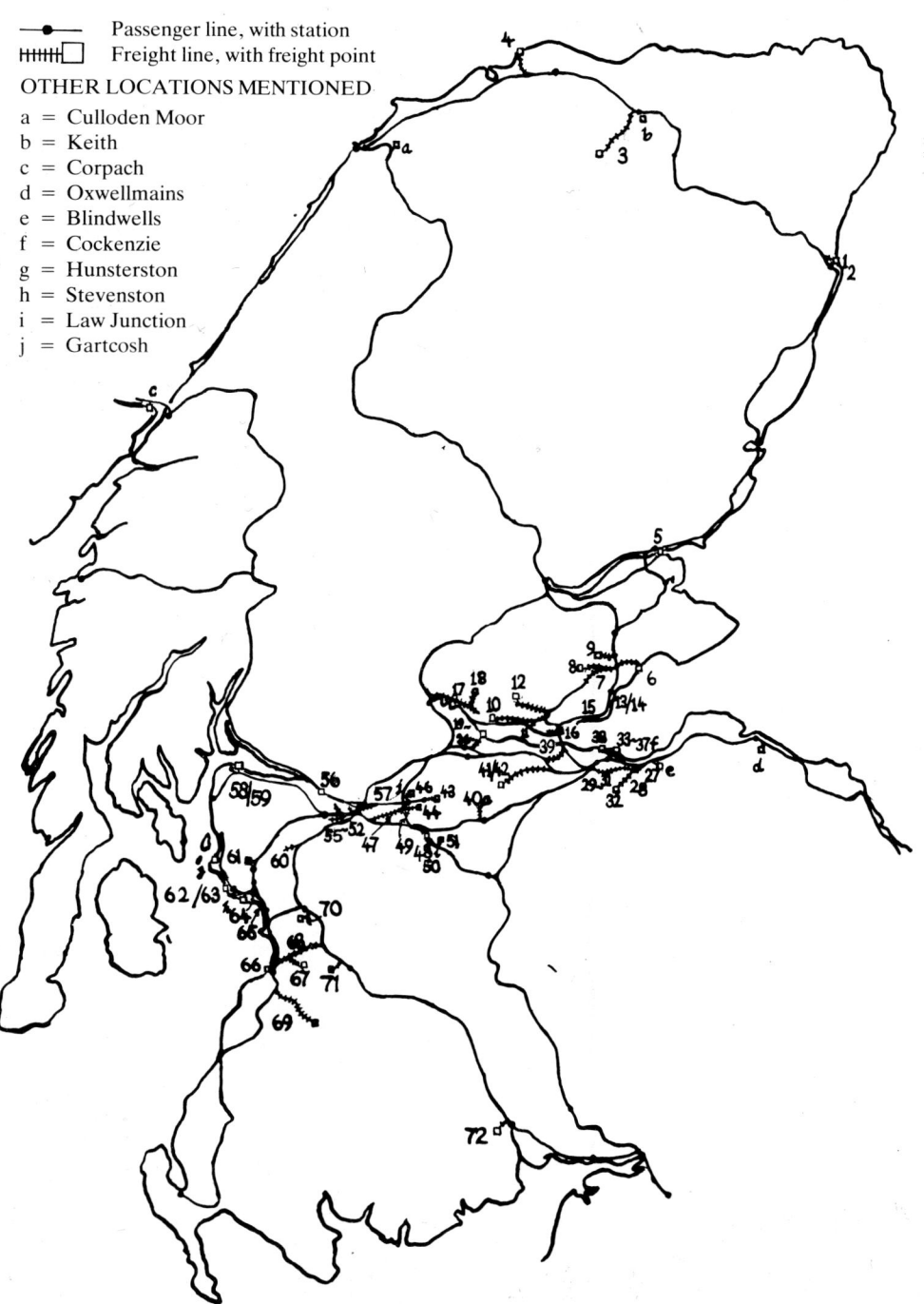

34. LOTHIAN. Leith Docks (Unitank Branch). OS66; NT279768.
This branch runs along the shore road on the north-east side of the Leith Docks Estate. On the morning of 27/8/1984, 08 575 was propelling loaded petroleum tanks to the tank farm. The wagons had arrived earlier on the 09.28 block train from Grangemouth (see 19). *(M. Macdonald)*

35. LOTHIAN. Leith Docks. OS66; NT277764.
Until the 1960s, many lines in Leith were still used for the transfer of freight around the Docks Estate, and from rail to ship. After the withdrawal of the D27xx class locomotives, the Class 08 shunters were officially not allowed to work to the mills at the Western Harbour. In July, 1981, a trip working from the Western Harbour to Leith South Goods was being hauled by a tractor. *(M. Macdonald)*

36. **LOTHIAN.** Abbeyhill Junction-Granton. OS66; NT236772. West Harbour Road, Granton on 26/9/1978, with 37 147 returning empty petroleum tanks to the Grangemouth refinery (see 19) from the Shell (U.K.) sidings. The terminal at Granton closed in 1980 and the branch is more or less "mothballed", being retained to allow access for very occasional trainloads of naphtha to Granton Gasworks.
(M. Macdonald)

37. LOTHIAN. Leith South Goods. OS66; NT284760.
On the afternoon of 8/6/1978, 26 001 was waiting to depart from Leith South Goods with one of the regular trips to Millerhill. The grain traffic from East Anglia, formerly carried by the COVHOP wagons (in the picture), is now carried in modern high-capacity bogie wagons. *(M. Macdonald)*

38. LOTHIAN. Leith South Junction (Portobello). OS66; NT303735.
A train of coated pipes from Leith South to Montrose is seen joining the main line at Leith South Junction on 27/7/1971 with 40 002 in charge. *(W. S. Sellar)*

39. **LOTHIAN.** Dalmeny Junction–Winchburgh Junction. OS65; NT135762.
The 17.55 Thornton-Mossend Speedlink train west of Dalmeny Junction on 21/8/1982 with 20 206 + 20 214 in charge. The train consists of an empty Tullis Russell china clay hopper (see 9) and wagons of wood pulp from Methil Docks (6) for Corpach. This is now part of the main freight route from the West of Scotland to Fife. As well as the daily Mossend-Thornton Speedlink feeder services, it carries regular trains of kerosene from Grangemouth to Leuchars, and is also used, as required, as a diversionary route for passenger trains.

(M. Macdonald)

40. & 41.   LOTHIAN.   Bathgate. OS65.

40. NS973685. A juvenile arsonist on a spree set fire to the former Bathgate station buildings some months before 46 037 was seen there on 29/1/1982, on arrival with a train of "Carflats" from King's Norton. *(M. Macdonald)*

41. NS982681. Some months later, 27 053 was leaving the Bathgate car terminal on 9/8/1983 with empty "Cartics" on the early morning return trip to Millerhill.
Rail-borne car deliveries are being concentrated at Bathgate with the transfer there, in 1984, of deliveries previously carried out from Elderslie (Strathclyde).
However, Bathgate is now much reduced as a railway centre; the sidings (left, background) have now been lifted, the coal yard (right) closed (1984), as have the short branch to the British Leyland factory and the freight-only line to Airdrie (43). *(M. Macdonald)*

42. LOTHIAN. Benhar Junction-Polkemmet Colliery. OS65: NS913623. A coal train for the Ravenscraig steelworks at Motherwell (see 50) climbs away from Polkemmet Colliery on 26/5/1982 with 20 078 and 20 063 in charge. (B. Roberton)

STRATHCLYDE REGION.   The Airdrie, Coatbridge, Mossend and Motherwell areas.
43.   Airdrie. Inverhouse branch. OS64; NS785658.
The branch to the Associated British Maltsters' mills at Inverhouse (near Airdrie) was re-opened in 1981. On the morning of 21/10/1983, 20 119 was leaving the exchange sidings for Mossend with empty grain hoppers. The line on the left (the former Airdrie-Bathgate line) was closed and lifted in 1982. Associated British Maltsters acquired a Class 08 to work between the mills and the exchange sidings.
(M. Macdonald)

44.   STRATHCLYDE.   Langloan Junction-British Steel Corporation Imperial Works. OS64; NS757645.
Gently does it! 20 154 comes gingerly down the spur from the Imperial pipe-coating works (Coatbridge) in the early afternoon of 8/5/1984 with a short train of pipes for Aberdeen (1).
   This is just one part of the inter-works steel traffic in the area; the pipes were manufactured at Mossend, nearby.
(M. Macdonald)

45. STRATHCLYDE. Whifflet-Coatbridge (Sunnyside)-Gunnie. OS64; NS736643.
On the afternoon of 8/5/1984, 20 154 left Whifflet for Mossend Yard with a daily trip working, including steel pipes collected earlier from Imperial Works (44) and a cement hopper wagon from the Gartsherrie cement works (46). The train is passing underneath the branch to the Imperial Works. *(M. Macdonald)*

46. STRATHCLYDE. Gartsherrie Cement Works, Coatbridge. OS64; NS727664.
The Clyde Cement shunter leaves Gartsherrie Works for the exchange sidings at Gunnie on the afternoon of 8/6/1984 with two loaded cement hoppers (see 45).
   The clinker used in the manufacture of the cement comes by daily block train from Clitheroe, Lancs., along with some finished product. After processing, the cement goes to Mossend Yard, from whence it is distributed to terminals in Northern Scotland. *(M. Macdonald)*

47. **STRATHCLYDE.** Rutherglen Junction-Rosehall Junction (Coatbridge). OS64; NS734643.
A Hunterston-Ravenscraig iron ore train approaching Rosehall Junction (Coatbridge) on the afternoon of 20/8/1981 with 37 154 + 37 137 in charge. The Calder branch (44) is on the embankment on the right.
   This is the main freight route out of Glasgow to Mossend and to the North. It avoids the busy passenger route through Uddingston and Motherwell. (See also 50, 52.)   *(M. Macdonald)*

48. **STRATHCLYDE.** Mossend South Junction-Ravenscraig Steel Works. OS64; NS759583.
Semi-finished steel products are moved short distances by rail between works in the Motherwell/Coatbridge area. On the morning of 14/10/1981, 37 151 was leaving the Ravenscraig Steel Works, Motherwell, with a train of steel coil for cold reduction at the nearby Gartcosh Strip Mill. (See also 22.)
   (M. Macdonald)

49. STRATHCLYDE.   Mossend Yard. OS64; NS749603.
Mossend is now Scotland's principal freight yard (Network Yard), handling the bulk of the Anglo-Scottish traffic on the Speedlink Network. On the afternoon of 8/5/1984, 85 030 was leaving for Carlisle. The leading wagon is an empty 57-tonne capacity china clay wagon. (cf 9!)   *(M. Macdonald)*

50. STRATHCLYDE.   Holytown Junction-Law Junction. OS64; NS775584.
This is the main route for freight traffic from Mossend to the South avoiding Motherwell. On 29/10/1980, 85 011 was on the mid-morning return Ravenscraig to Hardendale (Shap) empty limestone hoppers train, seen here near Carfin village. The line is also used by iron ore and coal traffic going into Ravenscraig steel works. (See also 40, 47.)   *(M. Macdonald)*

51. STRATHCLYDE. Garriongill Junction-Coltness. OS65; NS817535.
The mid-day trip from the Coltness works (a train of concrete-sleepered track) approaches Garriongill Junction on 8/6/1984 with 20 205 in charge. *(M. Macdonald)*

STRATHCLYDE. Glasgow (South Area).
52. Larkfield Junction. OS64; NS587633.
Larkfield is a busy junction which handles the freight traffic from the west and south-west of Glasgow (via Shields Junction, right, and Muirhouse Junction, curving left). In the mid-afternoon of 10/8/1984, 20 083 + 20 065 were coming east from Shields, heading for Mossend, with a trip from the Salkeld Street Freight Terminal. This route is also used by the Hunterston-Ravenscraig ore trains. *(M. Macdonald)*

53. **STRATHCLYDE.** General Terminus. OS64; NS576643.
Until the opening of the Hunterston ore terminal in Ayrshire in 1979, General Terminus Quay in the centre of Glasgow handled the iron ore for the Ravenscraig steel works.
Latterly, the site has been used for handling shale spoil from West Lothian (used by the construction industry), and 37 157 + 37 129 were on a train of empties leaving for West Lothian on the morning of 22/2/1980. However, this traffic ceased at the end of 1984.
(*M. Macdonald*)

54. STRATHCLYDE.   Deanside. OS64; NS528653.
Deanside is a rail/road "break-bulk" depot (see also 24), adjacent to the M8 Motorway. (Similar depots are operating at Law Junction, Mossend and Gartcosh.)
   37 152 was leaving Deanside in mid-afternoon of 9/3/1984 with a daily working to Mossend, conveying empty grain wagons for East Anglia. There is also daily vanload traffic. The track on the right leads to Shieldhall Docks, but is little used.
(M. Macdonald)

55. STRATHCLYDE.   Paisley (Hawkhead). OS64; NS482634.
The last traffic on the truncated Paisley (Canal) loop is petroleum from Grangemouth (19) to the Hawkhead terminal. At lunchtime on 6/1/1983, 37 264 ran round its train at Canal and returned to Grangemouth with empty tanks. The train "runs as required". The passenger service on the loop was withdrawn at the end of the same week. Latterly, "running round" has taken place at Hawkhead (NS502635).
(M. Macdonald)

STRATHCLYDE. Glasgow (North Area).
56. Dalmuir Riverside Branch. OS64; NS483712.
Empty whisky tanks, returning to Keith, were being propelled along the Dalmuir Branch by 26 023 in the early afternoon of 21/6/1984. Dalmuir is Chivas Brothers' principal bottling and blending plant. The whisky comes in regularly from Keith in bulk tanks; there is also van traffic from the plant. The train is passing the site of the former Caledonian Railway Dalmuir Riverside station, closed to passengers in October 1964.
(M. Macdonald)

57. STRATHCLYDE.   High Street Junction. OS64; NS604649.
Only kidding! There was an unusual freight working through the Glasgow Queen Street (Low Level) tunnels on 20/3/1981 when 27 112 was seen passing High Street Goods (closed 1982). Some of the Dalmuir-Keith workings (56) occasionally take this route. The freight-only connection to the south of the Clyde at Shields Junction is in the left foreground. *(M. Macdonald)*

58. STRATHCLYDE.   Greenock Docks. OS63; NS 301755.
This branch drops steeply and in a sharp 180 degree curve from the Ladyburn Yard to the United Molasses siding at James Watt Dock.
  08 447 is seen descending the branch with empty wagons on 24/10/1983 (mid-morning). The train will then set back about 100 yards to the United Molasses siding. Loaded molasses tanks are forwarded (more or less daily) to Glenochil Distillery, Menstrie (18). *(M. Macdonald)*

59. STRATHCLYDE.   Greenock (Princes Pier branch). OS63; NS281754.
This branch from the Port Glasgow-Wemyss Bay line serves the Clyde Port Authority Container Terminal at Princes Pier. 37 117 was passing the site of Lynedoch station in the mid-afternoon of 13/8/1984 with a daily working of container flats.   *(M. Macdonald)*

STRATHCLYDE. Ayrshire.
60.   Lugton-Giffen. OS63; NS365509.
The weed-killing train was seen near Barrmill on 7/6/1984; it was being propelled by 26 025.
(D. Blades; M. Macdonald Collection)

61.   STRATHCLYDE.   Dalry (Roche Products). OS63; NS304506.
The Vitamin C factory is served by a short branch from the Glasgow-Ayr line, just north of Dalry; the branch was opened in 1982 with the help of a grant under Section 8 of the Railways Act (1974).
   In the early afternoon of 10/5/1984, the Company's Barclay shunter was propelling fuel tanks into the works; these had been delivered earlier by the trip working from Ayr. Other inward traffic includes coal, salt and caustic soda.
(M. Macdonald)

62. STRATHCLYDE. Ardrossan (Shell Bitumen Refinery). OS63 or 70; NS232427.
On the last day of the "Ardrossan Pilot" (10/5/1984), the pilot, 08 430, was propelling bitumen tanks from the Shell Refinery to Ardrossan Yard. The train consisted of wagons which were later forwarded by Speedlink service from Ayr to Elswick (Newcastle), and a block train of tanks for Culloden Moor. Main line locomotives now perform this "trip" working.
    The platforms on the left of the picture are all that remains of the ex-Caledonian Railway "North" station, which closed in 1967. *(M. Macdonald)*

63. The Shell Barclay fireless locomotive taking a rest at the Ardrossan Refinery on the morning of 10/5/1984. *(M. Macdonald)*

64. **STRATHCLYDE.** Dubbs Junction-Byrehill Junction. OS63 or 70; NS296424.
This chord is used by chemicals trains working between the I.C.I. plant at Stevenston and plants at Haverton Hill (Teesside) and Fleetwood. In June, 1984, the weed-killing train, with 27 066 at the front, was heading for Byrehill Junction on its way south to Ayr. *(D. Blades; M. Macdonald Collection)*

65. **STRATHCLYDE.** Snodgrass, Bogside. OS70; NS307407.
This short branch goes off the Glasgow-Ayr main line just over a mile south of Byrehill Junction (see 64, above). On the morning of 10/5/1984, 20 039 was leaving with the daily return trip to Falkland Junction, Ayr. *(M. Macdonald)*

66. STRATHCLYDE.   Ayr Harbour. OS70; NS334229.
Not the usual photo of two Class 20s from the bridge outside the Scottish Agricultural Industries works, but 08 442 shunting coal hoppers on the quayside at Ayr on 6/9/1983. The coal, from Killoch colliery, was being loaded for Belfast by conveyor (left background).
   The last link with the old method of coal handling (hoisting the wagons individually and tipping their contents into the ship) is the crane in the foreground, retained, until recently, for domestic coal shipped to the Western Isles.
(M. Macdonald)

67. STRATHCLYDE.   Annbank Junction-Killoch Colliery. OS70; NS412235.
The predecessors of the Class 20s and the bottom-discharge coal hoppers (66) were the ex-Caledonian Railway 3F 0-6-0s and (often) non-vacuum-braked, end-tipping wagons.
   On 11/5/1961, 57633 + 57611 were seen approaching Annbank Junction with a train for Ayr Harbour on what is now the Killoch line.
(J. Currie)

68. **STRATHCLYDE.** Newton Junction-Annbank Junction-Mauchline Junction. OS70; NS417248.
This is a steeply graded line from Ayr to the Glasgow-Kilmarnock-Carlisle line at Mauchline. Just east of Annbank Junction, Mossblown, "Clan" 4-6-2 72001 was working hard uphill on 21/4/1962 with the Glasgow-Ayr-Carlisle parcels train.

This line was rumoured to be earmarked for closure late in 1984; traffic to be diverted by the Barassie-Kilmarnock route. *(B. Hamilton)*

69. **STRATHCLYDE.** Dalrymple Junction-Waterside. OS70; NS407139.
On 26/9/1960, "Austerity" 2-8-0 90319 was at Holehouse Junction, working from Ayr up to Waterside with empty coal wagons. This line leaves the main Ayr-Stranraer line a mile or two south of Ayr.
(J. Currie)

72. **DUMFRIES & GALLOWAY.** Dumfries, Maxwelltown branch. OS84; NX955764. The Maxwelltown branch is all that remains of the former Dumfries-Stranraer railway, closed in 1965. 25 230 was on the daily early morning trip from I.C.I. Cargenbridge on 12/6/1984, seen here passing the former Maxwelltown station. The small oil terminal on the right receives one train of tanks a week (as required) from Grangemouth (see 19). *(M. Macdonald)*

70. **STRATHCLYDE.** Kilmarnock (Riccarton). OS70; NS434365.
This short branch, which leaves the Kilmarnock-Carlisle line just south-east of Kilmarnock station, now serves a small tank farm at Riccarton which sees occasional oil traffic from Grangemouth. The line has now been cut back from Riccarton and Craigie, where ex-L.M.S. "Crab" 2-6-0 42743 was shunting on 6/4/1962.
(W. S. Sellar)

71. **STRATHCLYDE.** Barony Colliery, near Auchinleck. OS70; NS530225.
Barony Colliery is near the Kilmarnock-Carlisle line, between Mauchline Junction and Auchinleck. 24 001 was at Barony with National Coal Board 0-4-0ST No. 16 on 26/12/1974.
(J. L. Stevenson)